taxidermy Goes Wild!

Many animals died in the making of this book...

taxidermy
Goes Wild!

Rob Colson

CASSELL ILLUSTRATED

An Hachette UK Company
www.hachette.co.uk

First published in Great Britain in 2020 by
Cassell, an imprint of Octopus Publishing Group Ltd
Carmelite House
50 Victoria Embankment
London EC4Y 0DZ
www.octopusbooks.co.uk

ISBN 978-1-78840-235-4

A CIP catalogue record for this book is available from the British Library.

Printed and bound in China

10 9 8 7 6 5 4 3 2 1

Written, researched, edited and designed by Tall Tree Limited

Publishing Director: Trevor Davies
Author and picture research: Rob Colson
Design: Jonathan Vipond
Assistant Editor: Sarah Kyle
Senior Production Manager: Peter Hunt

contents

Introduction

At first glance, the world of taxidermy may seem a bit, well, stuffy. Dedicated experts, with detailed knowledge of biology and anatomy, labour away behind the scenes in museums to recreate life-like animals and give us an idea of how they lived. Well forget about all that business. There is a new breed of taxidermists in town who have said "Stuff That! We're going to show you animals as they have never looked or lived before". These taxidermists give their animals clothes. They put them on bicycles. They turn them into acrobats and sports stars. They transform them into figures from mythology. And they mix and match to make brand-new creatures. Pigs will finally fly!

Taxidermy first went wild in Victorian times. In the 1850s, strange dioramas began to appear in a pub in the sleepy English village of Bramber. The publican's son, Walter Potter, had dabbled in taxidermy as a boy in an attempt to preserve his much-loved pet canary. As he practised his art, Potter let his imagination run amok, creating scenes filled with animals in distinctly human poses and predicaments, from kittens at a wedding to rabbits in a classroom. Following his lead, Victorian taxidermists started to produce all manner of anthropomorphic scenes. Potter himself opened a museum to display his weird and wonderful dioramas.

Fast-forward to the early 2000s, and taxidermy took a bold step into the absurd with the Rogue Taxidermy movement. Stuffed animals started to appear in fashionable New York art galleries. This new generation of artists thought nothing of messing with nature, combining body parts to create flying goat-fish creatures or three-headed mice. And why not? While traditional taxidermists labour to produce life-like scenes, the rogue taxidermists were solely concerned with their own imaginations. And what rich – some might say warped – imaginations they were! These were scenes from the carnival, post-mortem freak shows of the fabulous and fantastic.

Today, many more taxidermists have taken to the internet to peddle their wares. Often they are entirely self-taught. If you want to have a scene created out of your twisted imagination, somebody out there will be more than happy to oblige. Is your heart set on a heavy metal band of grasshoppers? No problem. What about sinister gang of hooligan-hamsters? Give them a couple of months, and it's yours. Maybe you will be inspired by the creations in this book. We've gathered together a selection of the wildest taxidermy out there, snapped *in situ* by incredulous travellers or placed up for sale by their proud creators. If you can think it, the chances are someone's stuffed it.

Kit academy
A Walter Potter original from the 19th century

animals
with attitude

Balancing act

Sozzled squirrel

Poker faces at the Toadstool Casino

Easy rider

Bear with a sore head

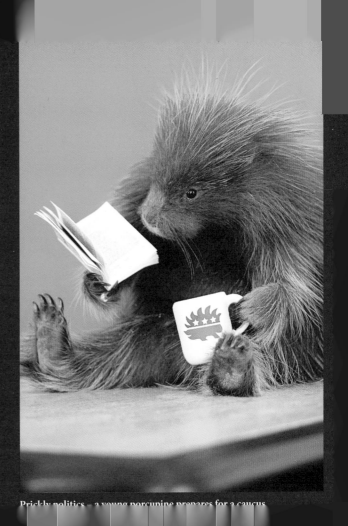

Prickly politics – a young porcupine prepares for a caucus

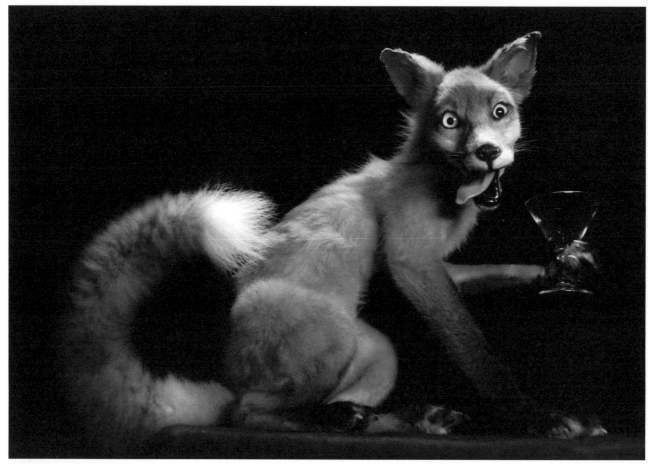

A frisky fox both shaken and stirred

"Show me the way to go home..."

Extreme urban foraging

What are you looking at?

Crumbs. Caught in the act again.

Not sure that's how you're supposed to hold a machine gun

Professor Brock

work
and play

Breakdancing skunk
From the crazy mind of Toronto's finest, Jeremy Johnson

Balancing ballerina – this pirouetting capybara spins on the spot!

Busking grasshopper

Disco opossum

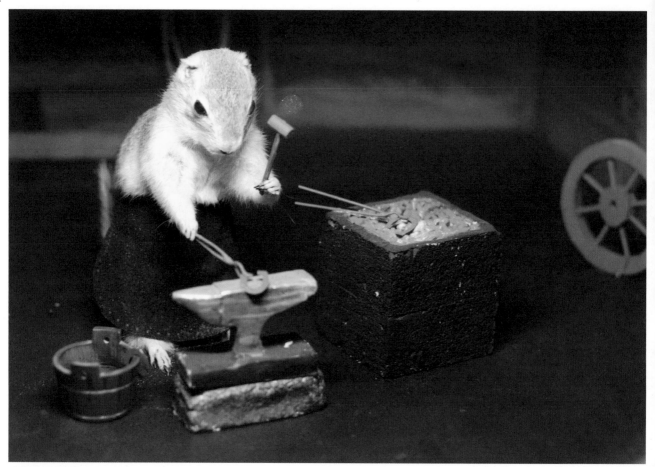

A gopher blacksmith makes shoes for a tiny, tiny horse

No-Clothes Friday at the office

An intrepid gopher trades the prairie for the jungle

Portrait of the artist as a young mouse

Harping guinea pig
Spotted in a Peruvian market. Next to the dried fish, naturally

Bongos? Check. Mandolin? Check. Ironic headgear? Check. It's the lesser-spotted hipster grey

A furry fiddler

Bavarian boogie

"Tah Dah!"

A virtuoso grasshopper on the violin

Lounge lizard

Cheers! Merry mice sharing tall tales, short tails and a pint

sporting
triumphs

Hunting in a high-vis? Good luck with that!

A gopher steps up to the plate

Putting the "chip" into "chipmunk"

Pint-sized pugilists

Head forward, body braced, this skunk is ready for the rapids

A lucky escape for this wave-riding beach rat

The Texans unveil their new wide receiver

Three members of the boating crew wondered who had let off the terrible stink

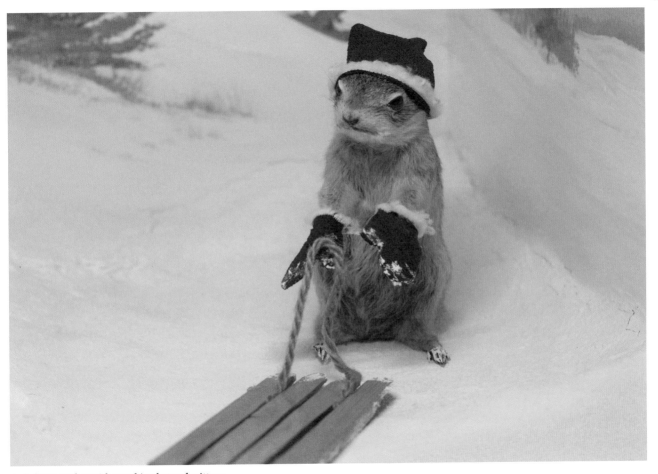

A sledging gopher with matching hat and mittens

Take the strain!

best-dressed
beasts

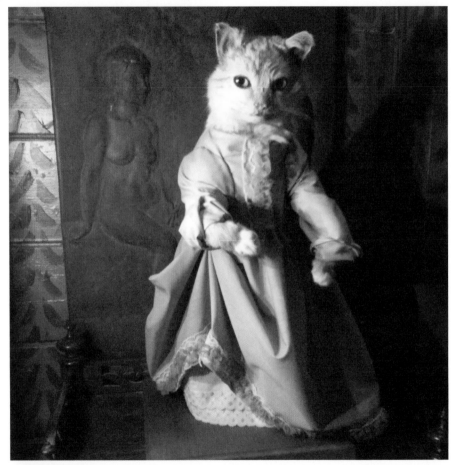

Fashionable feline
An elegant kitty, spotted at the Zetter Townhouse Hotel in London

Crow in mourning

Duck in a dickie bow

Ermine nun

A fancy frog puts his best foot forward

Who killed Bambi?

Complex Napoleon?

54

The squirrel pope blesses his flock

Audrey Hepburn with attitude

Grin and bear it

Unveiled: a veiled Edwardian lady squirrel

The Kittens' Wedding
Another strange scene from Walter Potter

Warrior fox, in his special warrior fox helmet with extra ear protection

"Alas, poor Mickey..."

This bear is standin', not Russian!

He's late! He's late! For a very important date!

Love-struck gophers sharing a moment

Holy crow, a corvid in a habit

domestic
bliss

Animal ablutions
A rodent from Haus of Mouse enjoying a soak

A nice cup of tea, reading glasses at the ready and a scarf to knit. Perfect

Tea should be drunk from a teacup, naturally

Interesting squat-on-the-seat technique there

Life after escaping the rat race

The dead commune with the even deader

Young master rabbit crams for his exams

out and
about

Hang on there, kitty!

Try getting to sleep after this guy has read you a bedtime story...

Smarter than the average bear in your pic-a-nic basket

Fly away, pretty bird!

Fox, hunting

No self-respecting fox hunts without a musical accompaniment

Think there might be a mole

Mouse on the Metro

Not sure this gopher will fit inside that train

Picnic thief

Opossum in springtime

house of
horrors

Mystic Mouse

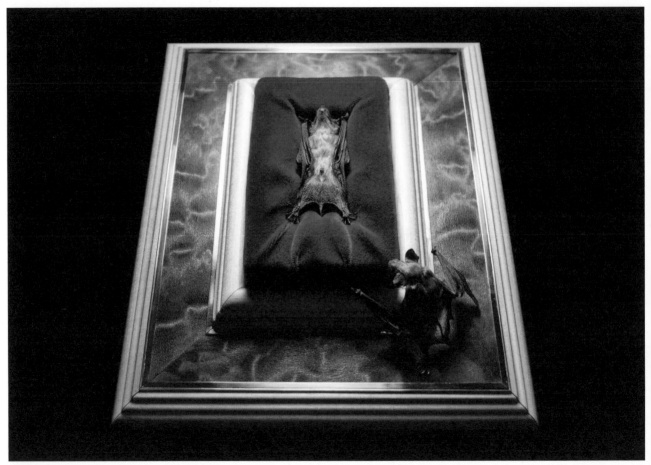

Bat wake
A macabre Gothic scene from Jeremy Johnson

Greek heroes take flight

"Why isn't it moving?" The cat is alive. And very confused

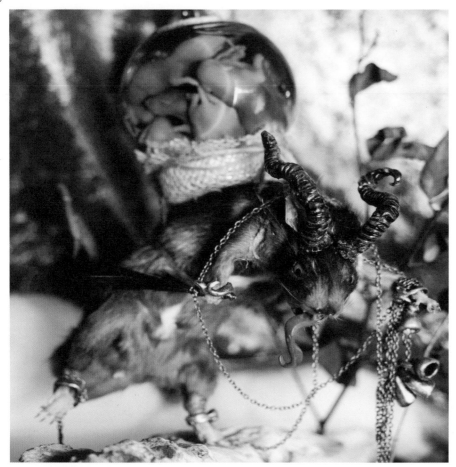

Half-goat (well, squirrel), half-demon, the Krampus punishes children who misbehave at Christmas

Feejee mermaid. This curiosity from the past was once a freak show staple, traditionally made from half-monkey, half-fish

Vampire bunny. Is that a reflection? Hmmm. Sus

Part-jackrabbit, part-antelope, it's a jackalope!

A crafty fox pulling some strings

Unicorn rat. With blue mohican and wings, like all the best unicorn rats

Zombie Squirrel. Death does not become her

Flying pigs
Out and about on parade in Toronto

"Shall I pay? No? Oh, ok then"

Acknowledgements

Image credits

Special thanks to:
10l, 11, 20, 25r, 31l, 31r, 32, 33l, 33r, 34, 42, 51r, 53, 59l, 92l Mario Broutin @ mbcreature
10r, 16r, 36, 39, 41, 80l Safari Works Décor
12, 16l, 17, 19, 30, 40, 43, 93 Rick Nadeau @ thesquirrelhole.com
13r, 14, 22l, 22r, 23l, 23r, 70, 72l, 72r, 74, 78l, 80r, 84, 88, 94 Jeremy Johnson @ Meddling with Nature
15, 18, 28, 64, 65, 66, 67, 68, 69 Haus of Mouse Taxidermy
25l, 26, 46, 49, 52, 56, 62, 85, 87l, 87r Livic's Taxidermy
54r, 92r Spookys Artwork
90l Jana Rose Arts

Additional credits:
8, 57, 75 Marc Hill/Alamy Stock Photo, 13l lightningfades @ Flickr, 24, 37, 45, 61 Alan Levine @ Flickr, 27 Eileenmak @ Flickr, 29 Lorna Mitchell @ Flickr, 38 acceptphoto/Shutterstock.com, 44 Emily Mathews @ Flickr, 48 Peter Burka @ Flickr, 50 tome213/Shutterstock.com, 51l, 78r, 82, 83 Brooklyn Taxidermy @ Flickr, 54l, 58 istolethetv @ Flickr, 55 Olga Zinovskaya/Shutterstock.com, 59r ID1974/Shutterstock.com, 60, 95 Michaelparkart/Shutterstock.com, 73 Oleg Elkov/Shutterstock.com, 76 Pavel Dzhunev/Shutterstock.com, 77 Ellena Bozhkova/Shutterstock.com, 79 Mack Male @ Flickr, 86 Engyles @ Flickr, 89 Cory Doctorow @ Flickr, 90r Paul Rich Studio/Shutterstock.com, 91 Robert Couse-Baker @ Flickr